Field Trip!

Grocery Store

Angela Leeper

Heinemann Library
Chicago, Illinois

© 2004 Heinemann Library
a division of Reed Elsevier Inc.
Chicago, Illinois

Customer Service 888-454-2279
Visit our website at www.heinemannlibrary.com

Designed by Kim Kovalick, Heinemann Library; Page layout by Que-Net Media
Printed and bound in China by South China Printing Company Limited.
Photo research by Jill Birschbach
08 07 06 05 04
10 9 8 7 6 5 4 3 2 1

Library of Congress Cataloging-in-Publication Data
Leeper, Angela.
  Grocery store / Angela Leeper.
      p. cm. – (Field trip!)
Includes index.
Summary: Introduces a typical grocery store, exploring what its employees do in the different departments out front and behind-the-scenes, and how customers pay for their purchases.
    ISBN 1-4034-5163-X (HC), 1-4034-5169-9 (Pbk.)
    1. Supermarkets–Juvenile literature. 2. Grocery shopping–Juvenile literature. [1. Supermarkets. 2. Grocery shopping.] I. Title.
    HF5469.L44 2004
    381'.456413–dc22

                                    2003014525

Acknowledgments
The author and publishers are grateful to the following for permission to reproduce copyright material:
p. 4 Robert Lifson/Heinemann Library; pp. 5, 8, 9, 10, 11, 12, 13, 14, 15, 16, 17, 18, 19, 20, 21, back cover Greg Williams/Heinemann Library; p. 6 Spencer Grant/PhotoEdit, Inc.; p. 7 Michael Newman/PhotoEdit, Inc.; p. 23 (T-B) Dennis Wilson/Corbis, Photodisc Red/Getty Images, Spencer Grant/PhotoEdit, Inc.

Cover photograph by Greg Williams/Heinemann Library

Special thanks to our advisory panel for their help in the preparation of this book:

Alice Bethke
Library Consultant
Palo Alto, California

Malena Bisanti-Wall
Media Specialist
American Heritage Academy
Canton, Georgia

Ellen Dolmetsch, MLS
Tower Hill School
Wilmington, Delaware

Special thanks to Weaver Street Market and Martin's Supermarket, South Bend, Indiana.

Contents

Some words are shown in bold, **like this.**
You can find them in the picture glossary on page 23.

Where Do We Buy Our Food?

We buy food at grocery stores.

Food is a kind of grocery.

There are other kinds of groceries, too.

Soap, toothpaste, and paper towels are groceries.

Where Do Groceries Come From?

The groceries come from farms or **warehouses.**

Trucks bring groceries to the store.

Truck drivers unload groceries
onto a **loading dock.**

Where Do They Keep the Groceries?

Foods that can spoil stay in a cooler.

It keeps food cool and fresh.

Other groceries stay in the stock room.

They stay here until there is room in the store.

Where Can You Find the Groceries?

aisle

shelf

Stockers put the groceries on shelves.

This aisle has shelves on both sides.

Some groceries are alike.

They are kept together
in departments.

What Is in the Produce Department?

The produce department has fruit and vegetables.

A scale shows the weight of this apple.

The price of the apple depends on how much it weighs.

What Is in the Dairy Department?

The dairy department has milk, butter, and cheese.

They must stay cold to stay fresh.

There is a cooler behind the milk.

This stocker is putting out more milk for people to buy.

What Is in the Meat Department?

The meat department has beef, chicken, and pork.

This deli worker cuts meat and cheese.

People can make sandwiches with them.

What Is in the Bakery Department?

The bakery has bread and cookies.

It also has cakes and pies.

Bakery workers make the bread.

The bread bakes in a big oven.

Where Do People Pay for Their Groceries?

People pay for their groceries at the checkout stand.

The **scanner** shows the prices.

cashier

cash register

People pay the cashier.

The money goes in the
cash register.

Grocery Store Map

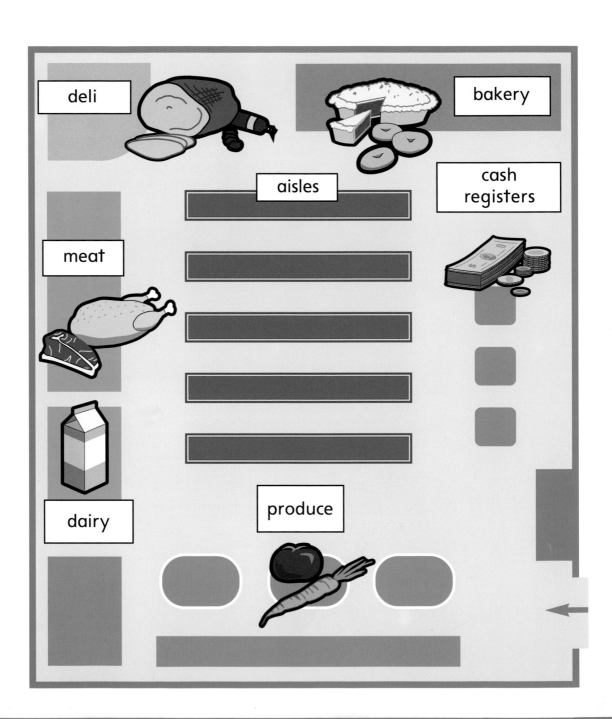

deli

bakery

aisles

cash registers

meat

dairy

produce

Picture Glossary

loading dock
page 7
place where things to be sold are brought into a store

scanner
page 20
machine that shows the price of something

warehouse
page 6
building where things are kept before they go to stores to be sold

Note to Parents and Teachers

Reading for information is an important part of a child's literacy development. Learning begins with a question about something. Help children think of themselves as investigators and researchers by encouraging their questions about the world around them. Each chapter in this book begins with a question. Read the question together. Look at the pictures. Talk about what you think the answer might be. Then read the text to find out if your predictions were correct. Think of other questions you could ask about the topic, and discuss where you might find the answers. Assist children in using the picture glossary and the index to practice new vocabulary and research skills.

Index